WOMEN'S ADORNMENT

What Does the Bible
Really Say?

by

Ralph Woodrow

International Standard Book Number: 0-916938-01-8.
Library of Congress Card Number: 76-17711.

A catalog of books and/or information
can be otained by contacting:

RALPH WOODROW
P.O. Box 21,
Palm Springs, CA 92263-0021

Toll-free Order/Message Line: (877) 664-1549
Fax: (760) 323-3982
Email: ralphwoodrow@earthlink.net
Website: www.ralphwoodrow.org

CONTENTS

1. SHOULD WOMEN WEAR SLACKS? 1

2. SHOULD WOMEN WEAR JEWELRY? 11

3. SHOULD WOMEN USE COSMETICS? 21

4. SHOULD WOMEN WEAR HEAD-COVERINGS? 29

5. SHOULD WOMEN CUT THEIR HAIR? 42

6. WOMEN'S MODEST APPAREL 47

Letters 55

INTRODUCTION

Within the framework of Christianity, certain questions have arisen concerning a woman's proper adornment. Must a Christian woman refrain from using makeup? Is she "worldly" if she wears earrings? Must she refrain from wearing slacks and wear only a dress? Is it a sin for a woman to cut her hair?

While such questions have not been major issues in most churches, still a significant number of people do consider these things as being of utmost importance. Others, though not directly involved in the controversy, are indirectly involved because of friends or relatives who are. All in all, there are multiplied thousands who have been confronted in one way or another with these questions.

I have met men who will not wear a tie clasp, wristwatch, wedding band, or shirt with short sleeves. I have met women who feel they must always wear some form of head-covering when attending worship services or offering prayer. Others have been told they would "go to hell" if they were to cut their hair or wear any makeup! Some wear only dull colored clothing. They would not think of wearing slacks, a ring, or earrings!

It is not easy to disagree with very fine and sincere people who hold such beliefs, especially when they feel these beliefs constitute a standard of holiness and spirituality. Nevertheless, in all good conscience it will be necessary for me to disagree with the strict and unfruitful extremism to which some have gone.

As Christians, we believe in a life of holiness. But "true holiness" (cf. Eph. 4:24) can never be that false holiness which consists merely in a set of rules—rules based on man-made traditions.

In Chapter One, the question of women wearing slacks is considered. The text commonly quoted in this connection—Deuteronomy 22:5—is examined *within its proper scriptural and historical setting.*

Chapter Two deals with the subject of jewelry. Does the Bible forbid the wearing of jewelry? Are things such as rings, earrings, necklaces, or bracelets wrong?

The Third Chapter goes into the questions surrounding the use of cosmetics. Should women refrain from using lipstick because Jezebel "painted her face"? What about powder, perfume, and eye shadow?

Chapters Four and Five provide a study on First Corinthians 11. Must a woman wear a head-covering during worship? Why did Paul say he had "no such custom"? Can a Christian woman cut her hair—or must it be left long and uncut? Is it a shame for a *man* to have long hair? Why did some men in the Bible have long hair?

Finally, we will seek to evaluate these things in the light of the overall spirit and attitude of Jesus as we pursue the question: What does the Bible really say?

—RALPH WOODROW
June, 2004

CHAPTER 1

SHOULD WOMEN WEAR SLACKS?

"The woman shall not wear that which pertaineth unto a man, neither shall a man put on a woman's garment: for all that do so are abomination unto the Lord" (Deut. 22:5).

For many years this verse has been the text for fervent sermons against women wearing slacks. Since the custom in our time is that men wear trousers, some have supposed that a woman who wears a garment that covers both legs and is divided in the middle has disobeyed the word of the Lord! With most who hold this view, it matters little if the woman is climbing a ladder, working in a garden, or taking part in sports activities. To them, only a dress is proper, and wearing slacks is wrong, is a sin, is un-Christian. A consistent study of Deuteronomy 22:5, however, will show that it has no reference to women wearing slacks.

We will hasten to point out that "transvestism"—the practice of a woman deliberately trying to appear as a man or a man trying to pass as a woman—is a deeply rooted and sad psychological problem. Such compulsive desire to dress like the opposite sex stems from a sexual abnormality. *But this is not the situation of women who wear slacks merely for the convenience they afford.* Neither is this the subject of Deuteronomy 22:5. The exchange of apparel in this verse refers to CULTIC transvestism. That is, men would dress as women and women as men in *worshipping heathen gods.* Those who did these things were an abomination to the Lord (Yahweh)—the word "abomination" being commonly linked with the worship of heathen gods (Deut. 12:31; 13:14; 18:12; 27:15; etc.). The practice involved idolatry and for this reason was strictly prohibited.

We may not be able to pinpoint exactly what all was involved in this false worship that existed during those days,

1

but a glance at some of the customs and superstitions that have developed during the centuries since then, can give us a *general* idea. Much of the following summary is taken from the scholarly *Hastings' Encyclopedia of Religion and Ethics* (Vol. 5, p.40).

From antiquity, says Plutarch, on the island of Cos, the priest of Heracles wore women's clothes when offering sacrifices. In harvest ceremonies in Bavaria the man in charge would dress as a woman; or, if a woman was in charge, she would dress like a man. In Rome, men who took part in the vernal mysteries dressed as women. In the Saturnalia festival, men exchanged clothes with women and slaves with their masters.

Those who were priests of the Zulu tribe wore the girdles of young girls when performing their rain-making ceremonies. A change in nature, they reasoned, required a change of their garments. Among the old Arabs, a man stung by a scorpion would put on a woman's bracelet and earrings to produce a cure; while in Central Australia a man might seek to cure his headache by wearing his wife's headdress.

Tacitus relates how the Nahanarvals, an ancient German tribe, had a priest dressed as a woman. Some peasant women in Germany wore their husband's coat at the time of childbirth "to delude the evil spirits." In Southern India, the wandering Erukalavandhu would put on some of his wife's clothing and retire to a dark room as she was giving birth to a child. Certain eunuchs in India who were dedicated to the goddess Huligamma wore female dress. Believing it was a sign of weakness to weep, the Lycians dressed as women when in mourning. The Patagonian sorcerers wore women's clothes. This practice was also known among various Indian tribes as a part of their rituals.

Men wore the clothing of women when they presented themselves before the Star of Venus; and women wore men's armor when presenting themselves before the Star of Mars. Idols were frequently represented with the features of one sex and the dress of the other. Sacrifices to Venus of Cyprus were made by men dressed as women and by women dressed as men. The practice was known among those of the cult of Leukippos in Crete. It was practiced by the worshippers of

2

Dionysus. Priests of Astarte, after castration, assumed female attire.

In sharp *contrast* to these rites, the worship of the true God did not require men to appear before him in women's apparel! Instead, being part of the worship of false gods, it was an abomination to the Lord. This was the real reason for the prohibition in Deuteronomy 22:5. In view of this, *this verse can hardly be considered a commandment against Christian women wearing slacks which are designed for women and worn for the convenience they afford.*

As believers in Christ and part of the *New* Testament church, we cannot rightly ignore the Old Testament. The early church did not. But, by the same token, we must realize that not everything in the Old Testament applies to Christians today. For example, the Old Testament says: "Build an ark." This, obviously, does not apply to us now. When the flood was coming, the command to build an ark was necessary; when the flood was over, the command no longer applied. It seems clear that Deuteronomy 22:5 was, likewise, given because of a specific situation at that time.

CONSIDER CONTEXT

Furthermore, it is always wise in the study of a verse to consider the *context*. Let us, then, consider other verses in this same chapter, as well as the chapters before and after it. It will be quite evident that the rules given in these chapters pertained to *a specific people and time*—not to *all* people at *all* times.

Deuteronomy 22:8 says that when one builds a new house, he is to make a "battlement"—a safety railing to protect someone from falling off the roof. When roofs were flat—when people spent time on their roofs and in some cases walked on them even from house to house—we can see the importance of a safety railing. But this same situation does not exist in most places today.

We are reminded of a story about a boy in a Bible class who read that David saw Bathsheba while walking on the roof of his house. Looking out the window and seeing the steep roofs that were common in his area, he asked: "What kept David from falling off the roof?" Not knowing any better, the teacher hastily replied: "Don't question the Bible, boy!" Upon hearing this, a teacher in an adjoining class leaned over and whispered to the teacher. "The answer to the difficulty is 'With men it is impossible, but not with God, for with God all things are possible'." Neither one had the *correct* answer!

Deuteronomy 22:11 says: "Thou shalt not wear a garment of divers sorts, as of woolen and linen together." Probably at that time there was a superstition that such mixing of materials had a magical effect. God's people were not to follow this practice—mainly because of it's association with heathen worship. No such situation exists today, however, and so there is no reason for not wearing clothes that may contain several kinds of material.

Deuteronomy 22:12 says: "Thou shalt make thee fringes upon the four quarters of thy vesture, wherewith thou coverest thyself." The word "fringes" here is translated "tassels" by Goodspeed, Moffatt, Rotherham, and others. Would any insist that this command was intended for us today? Who does it?

Deuteronomy 22:13-21 gives rules about handling the report of a man who claims he married a woman and found her not a virgin. A cloth—the token of virginity—was to be spread before the men of the city. If the husband was not telling the truth, he had to pay a fine; but if he was telling the truth, the girl was to be stoned to death!

Deuteronomy, chapter 23, begins by omitting certain ones from the congregation of the Lord. A reading of the opening verses plainly shows that such does not pertain to the gospel era. Later in this chapter, rules were given regarding sanitation. Since the invention of the toilet and sewer systems, practices such as those described in verses 12 and 13 are no longer required.

SELLING DOGS?

Verses 17 and 18 provide an interesting example of how a misunderstanding has resulted from a failure to examine the setting. "There shall be no whore of the daughters of

Israel, nor a sodomite of the sons of Israel. Thou shalt not bring the hire of a whore, or the price of a *dog*, into the house of the Lord." I can remember as a child hearing people say the Bible was against selling dogs, supposing the word "dog" used here was an animal that one might buy for a pet!

There have been cases in which people have been criticized for selling dogs, or churches have been criticized for accepting money from people who did. But this is not the point at all. The "dog" mentioned in this text is equivalent to a "sodomite," a male prostitute, the term being descriptive of their manner of copulation. In heathen practices, money was paid to sacred prostitutes, male and female, and this in turn went into the treasury of the cult temple. Such practices were an "abomination" to God. The hire of a whore or the price of a dog was not to be placed in the treasury of the Lord.

Looking now at the chapter just before our text, chapter 21, we notice that verses 1-9 give rules that were to be followed if someone was murdered and there was no suspect. The elders of the city were to take a heifer into a rough valley where no crops were planted and strike off it's head. Thus the land would be ridded of guilt. Would any insist that this ritual be followed today?

Deuteronomy 21:10-14 gives regulations about captives taken in war. If one happened to be a "beautiful woman," a soldier could take her home; she would shave her head and mourn for her parents a full month. "And after that thou shalt go in unto her, and be her husband...and it shall be, if thou have no delight in her, then thou shalt let her go"!

In cases such as this, the man might already have other wives. Polygamy was not uncommon. The verses that follow speak about laws of inheritance when a man had two wives. Regardless of which wife he loved or hated, his firstborn son was to receive a double inheritance. Would any make this an inflexible rule for our time? Must a firstborn son be given twice as much as the others?

Deuteronomy 21:18-21 states that if "a stubborn and rebellious son" will not obey his parents, they are to bring him to the elders of the city and announce that he will not obey; that he is "a glutton and a drunkard." Then "all the men of his city shall stone him with stones that he die"!

Now, with the context of Deuteronomy 22:5 in mind, I ask: if these other things do not apply to us today, how can people honestly take this one verse and try to make it a dogmatic law for Christians in our time? If these other things were never intended as laws for our time, is it not inconsistent to grab this one verse out of its setting and attempt to build a doctrine on it?

Over the years we have seen numerous little tracts which quote Deuteronomy 22:5—followed by comments that would make women who may occasionally wear slacks appear as a batch of ungodly sinners! Never once have I seen one of these tracts that ever attempted to explain why this taboo was given or to show it within its context!

Actually, there is more difference in men's and women's clothing today (even with slacks as part of women's apparel), than when all wore robe-type garments. When God made garments for Adam and Eve, there is no indication that he made a skirt for Eve and trousers for Adam. If there was any distinction at all between the garments he made, we are not told what it was. In later Bible times, whatever differences existed between the clothing of a man and that of a woman, it was not a contrast between trousers for the man and a skirt for the woman.

A MAN'S SKIRT?

The word "skirt" appears 12 times in the Bible (King James Version) and each time refers to the skirt of a MAN! We read about "the skirt of him that is a Jew" (Zech. 8:23); the skirt of the priest's garment (Hag. 2:12); the skirt of a father (Deut. 22:30); Saul's skirt (1 Samuel 24:4,5); the skirt of Boaz (Ruth 3:9); and, figuratively, the skirt of the Lord himself (Ezekiel 16:8).

The word "skirts" (plural) appears seven times (King James Version), translated from various words, and is used of men and women. It is evident that both sexes wore robe-type garments. Notice the clothing worn by the Old Testament high priest in the accompanying illustration.

6

JEWISH HIGH PRIEST

Something else should be noticed about Deuteronomy 22:5. The word "man" appears in the book of Deuteronomy about 78 times. It is usually translated from *iysh* (meaning man, a male) and a few times from *adam* (meaning mankind). BUT in Deuteronomy 22:5 the word translated "man" is from an *entirely different Hebrew word!* It is *geber*, meaning a warrior, a soldier. Bearing this in mind, the passage reads as follows: "The woman shall not wear that which pertaineth unto a soldier, neither shall a soldier put on a woman's garment." We have a contrast in this verse—not merely between the clothing of men and women—but between that which pertained to men of war (soldiers) and women.

In primitive cultures, times of battle were special times to seek the favor of their gods—the exchanging of garments being one of the magical rites in this connection. This may explain why Josephus, when quoting the warning in Deuteronomy 22:5, put it down as follows: "Take care *especially in your battles,* that no woman use the habit of man, nor man the garment of a woman" *(Josephus,* Book 4, 8:43).

Adam Clarke, a noted Biblical expositor, has commented on this verse as follows: "...*keli geber,* the instruments or arms of a man. As the word *geber* is here used, which properly signifies a man of war, it is very probable that armor is here intended; especially as we know that in the worship of Venus, to which that of Astarte or Ashtaroth among the Canaanites bore a striking resemblance, the women were accustomed to appear in armor before her. *It certainly cannot mean a simple change of dress, whereby the men might pass for women, and vice versa. This would have been impossible in those countries where the dress of the sexes had but little to distinguish it, and where every man wore a long beard."*

Lest there be any misunderstanding, I assure you that I think women should look like women and men should look like men. But the way this principle finds expression will vary from place to place and from age to age. Once we understand Deuteronomy 22:5 in its proper setting, it is clear that the Christian woman can make her decision as to what she should wear *as a woman*—not on the basis of a dogmatic and inflexible law—but within the framework of Christian liberty. This removes the problem from the sin realm, and makes it, instead, a matter of what is appropriate or proper. Being a non-essential point, whether a woman wears slacks is up to her as an individual. The one who wears slacks should not condemn the one who doesn't; and the one who doesn't should not condemn the one who does (cf. Romans 14).

Bicycle riding has become increasingly popular—not only for exercise or recreation—but as an alternative to the use of the family car for short errands. For this, slacks are more appropriate and practical than a dress. Such is also true with many other sports activities in which women take part. Many examples could be given.

CONSIDER THE FRUIT

The principle that we can know a tree by the kind of fruit it bears might well apply here. I believe I have seen this problem from many sides. I can truthfully say I have never seen any good fruits come from the strict, over-emphasis that some have tried to force into Deuteronomy 22:5. It has caused an unnecessary confusion in the homes and churches in which it has been taught. It has encouraged judging, strife, and a Pharisee spirit. It has never promoted a radiant Christian testimony. The inconsistency involved in many situations has hindered it.

I know parents who will not allow their teen-age daughters to wear anything but dresses in their gym classes at school. Consequently, if these girls take part in sports activities in dresses, they feel out of place; if they sit at the sidelines and don't take part, as is often the case, they feel out of place. I have known of young people who have become discouraged and have actually quit school to avoid the embarrassment.

I know women who work on outdoor jobs in cold weather. Something to cover their legs would be much more comfortable and practical, but for fear they will "lose out with God," they wear only dresses.

One young lady who worked in a department store was required occasionally to climb ladders to take inventory. To do this (with customers passing below) in a dress would hardly be proper. To wear slacks was against her religion. So what did she do? She gave up the job—even though she needed the work.

Back in the 60s I knew a young minister who was dismissed from his position in a certain denomination because someone spotted his wife in slacks! Actually, the slacks for the occasion were more appropriate than a dress would have been. But religious dogma, unfortunately, causes some people to no longer think. They have been taught that things are a certain way—and they refuse to consider the situation, the background of a Biblical statement such as Deuteronomy 22:5, or the reason *why* it says what it does.

We should respect the sincere convictions of people, of course—even though we may disagree with them. But a person who insists on using Deuteronomy 22:5 as a text (out of context) against slacks, had better be sure his own suit is not made of more than one kind of material. And, he should make sure he is wearing four tassels on his garment!—things also mentioned in this chapter. Let us, at least, be consistent.

CHAPTER 2

SHOULD WOMEN WEAR JEWELRY?

"Here is the formula of failure," says a tract sent to me some months ago. "First allow engagement and wedding rings, then school and class rings and pins, then other jewelry with sentimental 'value,' then jewelry in every form, all the way from that sold in the five and ten to that in the first-class jewelry store...open up the gate to one kind of ring, and it will be very difficult to stop at that point. If mother wears a wedding ring, how can she object to her daughter wearing a class ring?"

According to such tracts, wearing jewelry will cause spiritual failure. Some have an obsession against rings—even a ring which symbolizes marriage! It becomes a major belief to them. Others will permit a ring on the *finger*, but feel that *ear*rings are "worldly." What does the Bible say about these things? The two passages which, supposedly, tell Christians not to wear jewelry are as follows:

First Timothy 2:9,10 says women should be properly adorned—"*not* with braided hair, or gold, or pearls, or costly array; but...with good works."

And,

First Peter 3:3,4 says a woman's adorning should "*not* be that outward adorning of plaiting the hair, and of wearing of gold, or of putting on of apparel; but let it be the hidden man of the heart...even the ornament of a meek and quiet spirit, which is in the sight of God of great price."

What many have failed to understand is that these verses are using a very common HEBREW IDIOM. An "idiom" is a manner of speaking distinctive of a certain

11

people or language. In this case, the idiom was a manner of speaking which would minimize a first clause in order to emphasize a second clause. Today, in order to express the thought contained in this type of idiom, we would place the word "only" in the first clause, and "also" (or perhaps "rather") in the second clause, as follows: "Let not a woman's adorning be (only) that of outward things—such as fixing her hair, wearing gold, or pearls, or apparel—but (also, rather) let it be the inward adorning of a meek and quiet spirit." With this, the emphasis is on the second clause, *but it does not do away with the first clause.* It is in addition to it.

BIBLICAL EXAMPLES OF IDIOM

We now ask the reader's patience as we cite many verses in which this idiom is used in the Bible. The *Pulpit Commentary* says it is "a *common* Hebraism" and quotes, for example, John 6:27: "Labor not for the meat which perisheth, but for that meat which endureth unto everlasting life." If we do not recognize the Hebrew idiom here, this verse would sound like a command not to work! But other verses say men should work for their food, they should provide for their families, etc. The actual thought, then, is that we should not work for the material necessities of life (only), but (also, rather) for that which will endure unto everlasting life.

Or notice Genesis 32:28: "Thy name shall be called no more Jacob, but Israel." The meaning is that his name would no more be called Jacob (only), but he would have another name (also, rather), the name Israel. The proof that this is the correct meaning is seen by the fact that he was called Jacob many times *after* this, even by God himself: "And God spake unto Israel...and said, Jacob, Jacob" (Gen. 46:2).

Joseph's brothers sold him into slavery, yet Joseph stated; "So now it was not you that sent me hither, but God" (Gen. 45:8). Understanding the idiom, it could be worded: "So now it was not you (only) that sent me here, but it was God (also, rather)"!

During the journey of the Israelites in the wilderness, we are told they murmured against Moses and Aaron (Exodus 16:2). But in verse 8 we read: "...your murmurings are not

12

against us, but against the Lord." Considering what was just plainly stated, we recognize the idiom: "Your murmurings are not against us (only), but against the Lord (also, rather)"!

When Israel rejected Samuel and cried out for a king, God said: "They have not rejected thee, but they have rejected me" (1 Sam. 8:7). Yet verse 8 shows that they had rejected Samuel. Again, it is the Hebrew idiom, the meaning being: "They have not rejected you (only), but they have rejected me (also, rather)."

The use of the idiom seems clearly indicated in the wording of Joel 2:13: "Rend your heart, and not your garments, and turn unto the Lord." Rending garments and putting on sackcloth (2 Sam. 3:31) was a common mourning custom. In view of this, the meaning of Joel was: "Rend not (only) your garments, but rend your heart (also, rather)"! The emphasis is thus on the heart, not on the outward forms of religion.

When Peter said he believed Jesus was *the Christ*, Jesus replied: "Flesh and blood hath not revealed it unto thee, but my Father which is in heaven" (Matt. 16:17). But Peter *had* heard this from "flesh and blood"—before he ever met Jesus. Peter's own brother had told him: "We have found the Messias, which is, being interpreted, the Christ" (John 1:41). All is clarified once we recognize the idiom. It was not flesh and blood (only) which had revealed this to him; it had been revealed to him (also, rather) by the Father!

In John 4:21-23, Jesus said that the hour was coming, and then was, that true worshippers would not worship at Jerusalem or in Samaria—that God must be worshipped in spirit and in truth. But after this men *did* worship God at Jerusalem (Lk. 24:52,53; Acts 2; etc.). Recognizing the idiom, we realize that people would not worship at Jerusalem (only), but (rather) in spirit and in truth—regardless of location.

Or look at Jesus' words in Mark 9:37: "Whosoever shall receive me, receiveth not me, but him that sent me." In our way of speaking, it would be: "Whosoever shall receive me, receiveth not me (only), but him that sent me (also, rather)." The use of the idiom is seen also in John 12:44: "He that believeth on me, believeth not on me, but on him that sent me."

When Lazarus was sick, Jesus said: "This sickness is not unto death, but for the glory of God" (John 11:4); that is, this sickness was not unto death (only)—death did not end this matter, for Lazarus was raised from the dead. Peter used the idiom when he spoke to Ananias: "Thou hast not lied unto men, but unto God" (Acts 5:4). Ananias did lie to men, but the emphasis is on the fact he lied to God. Thus we could say: "You have not lied unto men (only)—your sin goes further than this—you have lied to God"!

Paul said: "I labored more abundantly than they all: yet not I, but the grace of God which was with me" (1 Cor. 15:10). Paul labored. This is clear. Yet to emphasize the grace of God, he used the idiom. John also used the idiom when he said: "Let us not love in word, neither in tongue; but in deed" (1 John 3:18). The context speaks about a brother in need. If we have this world's good and do not help him, we do not really have love. We can *tell* him we love him—we can love in *word*—but this is not enough. Thus the instructions: "Let us not love in word (only), but (also, rather) in deed."

In Luke 14:12-14, we read: "When thou makest a dinner...call not thy friends, nor thy brethren...but call the poor, the maimed, the lame, the blind..." The idiom makes the first part into a strong negative in order to emphasize the second part. The meaning is, "Call not (only) your friends, but (also, rather) the poor, blind," etc. If this was a command not to call friends to supper, why did Jesus accept invitations to eat with his friends? Friends and relatives eating together, even having feasts, was quite common in the Bible.

A comment in the *Cambridge Greek Testament* on this verse says: "We must take into account the idioms of Oriental speech...the 'not' means, as often elsewhere in Scripture, 'not only...but also' or 'not so much...as'." This work cites other examples of the idiom, including the text regarding jewelry, 1 Timothy 2:9.

With these things in mind, we look again at our text and it will be clear that jewelry was not forbidden: "...whose adorning let it not be [only] that outward adorning of plaiting

14

the hair, and of wearing of gold, or of putting on of apparel, but [also, rather] let it be the...ornament of a meek and quiet spirit." The emphasis is on the inward adorning, but the outward adorning is not eliminated.

NO APPAREL?

Evidence that we are dealing with an idiom may be seen right within the text. *If* the words about plaiting the hair, wearing gold, and putting on apparel meant a woman could not fix her hair and could not wear *any* jewelry, then it would also mean she COULD NOT WEAR ANY APPAREL! All of these things are included in the same statement (1 Peter 3:3,4).

To put it another way, unless we recognize the use of the Hebrew idiom, the following *absurdities* would be a summary of Biblical commandments or statements. Joseph's brothers did not send him to Egypt. Israel did not murmur against Moses. Israel did not reject Samuel. People who receive Christ do not receive him. People who believe in Christ do not believe in him. Ananias and Sapphira did not lie to Peter. Paul did not labor in the gospel work. Lazarus did not die. Do not speak kind words. Do not work for a living. Do no invite friends to supper. Women should not wear clothing.

"IN OLD TIME..."

If these two verses (1 Timothy 2:9 and 1 Peter 3:3) are not expressing an idiom—but are actually forbidding the use of jewelry—then they are CONTRARY TO ALL THE REST OF THE BIBLE ON THIS SUBJECT! Following the reference in First Peter, we read: "For after this manner in old time the holy women...adorned themselves," Sarah obeyed Abraham, etc. (1 Peter 3:5,6). Going back to those days "in old time," did the women wear jewelry? Indeed they did.

When Abraham's servant was sent to seek a wife for Isaac, he presented Rebekah with "a golden earring...and two bracelets for her hands...and the servant brought forth jewels of silver, and jewels of gold, and raiment, and gave them to Rebekah: he gave also to her brother and to her mother precious things" (Gen. 24:22,47,53). There is not the slightest hint that such presents were "worldly," sinful, or out of place. Instead, they are mentioned in a very good sense. There was nothing wrong about Rebekah wearing gold! Sarah, no doubt, also wore jewelry. Would Abraham send jewels for Rebekah and leave his own wife unadorned?

Judah—from whom the tribe of Judah gets its name—wore a "signet," probably a ring worn on a finger or suspended from the neck, as well as "bracelets" (Gen. 38:18). Joseph, highly esteemed in Biblical history, wore a "ring" (given to him by the king of Egypt) and "a *gold* chain about his neck" (Gen. 41:42). Mordecai was given a ring by king Ahasuerus (Esther 8:2). Saul wore a bracelet (2 Sam. 1:10). King Belshazzar gave Daniel scarlet clothing and "a chain of *gold* about his neck" (Dan. 5:29). In none of these cases is there any idea that wearing jewelry was displeasing to God.

When Israel came out of Egypt (sometimes regarded as a type of forsaking the world and worldliness), God did not command them to take off their jewelry in order to find favor with him. Later, when they fell into idolatry and wanted a golden calf, Aaron told them: "Break off the golden earrings, which are in the ears of your wives, of your sons, and of your daughters...and *all* the people broke off the golden earrings" (Exodus 32:2,3). We notice from these words that all of the Israelites wore golden earrings—both men and women. Their removal had not been ordered by God, but was ordered by Aaron.

During a time of mourning, we read that "no man did put on him his *ornaments*" (Exodus 33:4), a situation which indicates that normally they did wear ornaments. Sometimes jewelry was even used as an offering unto the Lord, as in Exodus 35:22.

The man who stood at the very center of Old Testament worship—the high priest—wore not only gold, but his garment was decorated with various jewels: sardius, topaz, carbuncle, emerald, sapphire, diamond, ligure, agate, amethyst, beryl, onyx, and jasper (Exodus 28:17-20).

Following Job's trial, his brothers, sisters, and others "gave him a piece of money, and every one an *earring* of gold.

So the Lord blessed the latter end of Job more than his beginning" (Job 42:11,12). Jewelry was part of the Lord's blessing upon Job and symbolized restored friendship.

In speaking of Saul's *good* points, not his bad ones, David spoke (as it were) to the daughters of Israel concerning Saul: "...who clothed you in scarlet, with other delights, who put *ornaments of gold* upon your apparel" (2 Sam. 1:24-27).

Isaiah 3:16-23 gives a list of ornaments worn by the women of Jerusalem which includes rings, earrings, bracelets, ornaments of the legs, and nose jewels. Judgment was pronounced upon Jerusalem. These things would be taken away. But this should not be misconstrued to teach that jewelry—as such—was considered evil in the sight of God. This is evident, for even things such as bread, water, bonnets, veils, and common clothing would also be taken away! The passage does, however, give us an insight into the customs of those times regarding clothing and jewelry.

In Song of Solomon 1:10 we read: "Thy cheeks are comely with *rows of jewels,* thy neck with *chains of gold.*" Some believe this book illustrates the love of Christ for the church. If so, surely the jewelry mentioned here is used in a very *good* sense, not a bad one.

The instruction of a mother and father to their son is called "an ornament of grace unto thy head, and chains about thy neck" (Proverbs 1:9). In Proverbs 25:12 we read: "As an earring of gold, and an ornament of fine gold, so is a wise reprover upon an obedient ear." Again, jewelry was used to typify good things.

Words of encouragement and blessing were directed by God to Zerubbabel, governor of Judah: "I...will make thee as a signet: for I have chosen thee, saith the Lord" (Hag. 2:23). He would be an object ever close to the Lord, as a ring is ever before the eye. Making Zerubbabel as a signet ring does not carry a bad meaning, but was a type of the Lord's blessing upon him. Likewise, in Malachi 3:17, God used jewelry to symbolize that which was good: "And they shall be mine, saith the Lord, in that day when I make up my *jewels;* and I will spare them."

In Ezekiel, the origin and history of Jerusalem was compared to a newborn baby that had been cast aside. No one else wanted her, but the Lord took her in and clothed her. She grew into a young woman and was given fine clothing to wear. "I decked thee also with *ornaments,*" God says, "and I put *bracelets* upon thy hands, and a *chain* on thy neck. And I put a *jewel* on thy forehead, and *earrings* in thine ears" (Ezekiel 16:11,12). This passage makes a very strong point. When the Lord drew this parallel, he used jewelry to symbolize his blessings upon Jerusalem. Now if things such as earrings and necklaces were forbidden by God, were unholy, were sinful—*how could they possibly make the point that was intended in this passage?* If these things were sinful, why is the *Lord* represented as the one who gave them?

That jewelry was highly regarded among God's people "in old time" is seen by the wording of Jeremiah 2:32: "Can a maid forget her *ornaments,* or a bride her attire?" In Revelation 21:2, we read about the holy city "as a bride *adorned* for her husband." This brief reference does not explain just what this adornment was, but the symbolism is doubtless based on Isaiah 61:10: "...as a bride adorneth herself *with her jewels*"! Now if wearing jewelry is a sin (as some extremists groups teach), how could the pure and undefiled bride be thus described? A bad thing does not symbolize a good thing. The holy city is further described as having gates of *pearl* (Rev. 21:21). If pearls were *unholy,* what place could they have in describing the *holy* city?

Those who interpret 1 Timothy 2:9 to mean that any wearing of pearls is wrong, face serious problems of interpretation. Take the words of Jesus in Matthew 7:6 for example: "...neither cast ye your pearls before swine." Pearls would represent things which are good, in contrast to swine—swine representing those who are unholy, unclean, evil. If wearing pearls was a sin in the sight of God, there would be no contrast or point in this saying of Jesus.

The wayward young man who repented and returned to his father's house, was given the best robe, a special supper, and "a *ring* on his hand" (Lk. 15:22). This story is commonly used to illustrate how God will welcome the sinner who forsakes the world and returns to Him. Obviously, then, if the wearing of a ring is sinful, the whole point of the story would be greatly weakened. If wearing a ring is wrong, the story should have said that the young man laid aside his ring (sin), and then returned to his father's house!

If God is against the use of jewelry, why would we find all of these references to jewelry in the Bible—in the New Testament as well as the Old Testament? If jewelry is *evil*, why was it repeatedly used in the scriptures as a type of things that were *good*? When there are strong reasons for believing that the statements found in 1 Timothy 2:9 and 1 Peter 3:3 are idioms, why should some try to give them a meaning that is contrary to everything else in the scriptures?

Israelite women wore jewelry on different parts of the body, even on the *nose.* "Nose jewels" (Isaiah 3:21) are sometimes explained as jewels hanging from the forehead to the upper part of the nose. However, as *Clarke's Commentary* (Vol. 4, p.37) points out, "It appears from many passages of Holy Scripture that the phrase is to be literally and properly understood of nose-jewels, rings set with jewels hanging from the nostrils, as ear-rings from the ears, by holes bored to receive them....This fashion, however strange it may appear to us, was formerly and is still common in many parts of the East, among women of all ranks."

In the days of Moses, mention is made of the people having "bracelets, and earrings, and rings, and *tablets,* all jewels of gold" (Exodus 35:22; Num. 31:50). The word here translated "tablets," means, according to Rashi, a noted Eleventh century Jewish commentator, "a golden object fixed on a woman's private part." In support of this view—which may or may not be correct—he quoted the words of certain rabbis as recorded in the Talmud. But the point we would make is this: considering all the uses of ornaments by women in the Bible, today's customs of wearing jewelry seem quite innocent and moderate in comparison!

If 1 Timothy 2:9 means that any wearing of gold is wrong, one wonders why gold rings were the subject of praise in Song of Solomon 5:14. Why did the Israelites—including the high priest—wear gold? Even men like Daniel and Joseph wore gold. If wearing gold is wrong, what about gold rimmed glasses or a gold filling in a tooth? If wearing gold is wrong, what about things which have a gold appearance—a belt buckle, wrist watch, or tie clasp? Should a policeman not wear a gold colored badge?

Sometimes, I fear, those who claim to be holiness people, while opposing the man-made traditions of the more formal churches, have made up traditions of their own that are equally unscriptural! It is not consistent to talk of *Bible* holiness and then make up rules that are not even in the Bible. So far as we know, Jesus said nothing against wearing jewelry, but he did expressly speak against *judging* (Matt. 7:1). Yet there are those who will sit in judgment concerning someone who wears jewelry and fail to realize that their *attitude* may be worse than the jewelry of those they condemn.

Are we saying, then, that Christians should rush out and buy a lot of jewelry? No, this is not the point. It is an individual matter. Taking everything into consideration, I feel—as with other things—we should avoid the extremes. As *Halley's Bible Handbook* (p. 594) states: "We do not understand [1 Peter 3:3,4] to prohibit a woman's desire to be attractive in personal appearance, but rather a caution against overdoing it, remembering that no amount of finery can be a substitute for a gracious Christian personality." Too much jewelry could detract from the inner beauty and appear overdone—even silly. On the other hand, God does not require a drab and dull appearance. Why shouldn't a woman try to look nice? If the motive of her heart is right, her efforts are not wrong.

CHAPTER 3

SHOULD WOMEN USE COSMETICS?

Churches which equate a plain look with salvation, commonly look with suspicion on women who wear makeup. After all, didn't wicked old Jezebel paint her face? Some feel that women who use makeup are "not saved." Others would not carry it this far, but would regard the use of makeup as a sign of low spirituality. Those who reluctantly allow makeup might say: "Well, a little paint helps an old barn." Others argue, however, that "when the barn catches on fire, all the paint peels off!" What does the Bible say about the use of things such as perfume, powder, and lipstick?

First, consider perfume. The use of perfume is generally acceptable—even by those who would frown on the use of lipstick. In Bible times, perfumes were highly regarded and used in a variety of ways. Men who made perfumes were called apothecaries; women who made perfumes were confectionaries (Ex. 37:29; Ecc. 10:1; 1 Sam. 8:13). References to perfume in one form or another are found from Genesis to Revelation.

In the days of Joseph, the "Ishmeelites came from Gilead with their camels bearing spicery and balm and myrrh, going to carry it down to Egypt" (Gen. 37:25). Gilead was the home of a number of fragrant shrubs and plants, including (as mentioned in this text) the "balm of Gilead" (Jer. 8:22).

Two of the most ancient recipes for perfume are found in the Bible. One perfume was made from sweet spices, stacte, onycha, galbanum, and frankincense—"a perfume...pure and holy" (Ex. 30:34-38). The other contained myrrh, cinnamon, calamus, and cassia (Ex. 30:22-33). These ingredients were mixed with oil and poured upon Aaron's head (Psalms 133:2). While this particular perfume was reserved for anointing the high priest, the general idea of using perfume could not be wrong or it would have been entirely out of place here.

That various perfumes and spices were held in high regard is repeatedly seen in the Song of Solomon:

"...my *spikenard* sending forth the smell thereof. A bundle of *myrrh* is my wellbeloved unto me....My beloved is unto me as a cluster of *camphire*" (1:12-14).

"Who is this that cometh out of the wilderness...perfumed with *myrrh* and *frankincense*, with all *powders* of the merchant?" (3:6).

"I will get me to the mountain of *myrrh*, and to the hill of *frankincense*....How fair is thy love...and the smell of thine *ointments* than all spices!" (4:6,10).

"The smell of thy garments is like the smell of Lebanon...*camphire*, with *spikenard*, and *saffron; calamus* and *cinnamon...frankincense; myrrh* and *aloes*, with all the chief spices" (4:13,14).

"I have gathered my *myrrh* with my spice...my hands dropped with *myrrh*, and my fingers with sweet smelling *myrrh*...his cheeks are as a bed of spices..." (5:1,5,13).

In Psalms 45:6-8, we read: "Thy throne, O God, is for ever and ever...all thy garments smell of *myrrh*, and *aloes*, and *cassia*, out of the ivory palaces." In Ecclesiastes 7:1, a "precious ointment" is likened to a good name. And Proverbs 27:9 says: "Ointment and *perfume* rejoice the heart: so doth the sweetness of a man's friend by hearty counsel." In all these references, perfume is used in a good sense; is likened to good things; is highly regarded!

Esther, commonly considered a great champion of women among the Jews, was perfumed for one year before she was taken unto the king—"six months with oil of myrrh, and six months with sweet odours" (Esth. 2:12,13)!

There are several references to perfumes in connection with Jesus. Following his birth, "frankincense and myrrh" were presented to him (Matt. 2:11). A very strong perfume was put upon Jesus when Mary took "a pound of ointment of spikenard, very costly, and anointed the feet of Jesus...and the house was filled with the odour of the ointment" (John 12:3). *Jesus* did not criticize this act; *Judas* did! When Jesus died, Joseph and Nicodemus wrapped the body in linen cloth with myrrh and aloes (John 19:39,40).

In view of these Biblical references, certainly today's use of perfume, cologne, shaving lotion, and things with a good smell, sensibly used, should not be questioned. Likewise, it is our opinion that a *sensible use of makeup is not contrary to the principles of the Christian faith.* None can rightly object to makeup on the basis that it is "adding to nature," any more than he could say that using perfume is adding to nature. The one simply has to do with appearance, the other with smell.

WHAT ABOUT JEZEBEL?

The usual argument against makeup, especially lipstick, is based on the verse which says that Jezebel painted her face. "And when Jehu was come to Jezreel, Jezebel heard of it; and she *painted her face,* and tired her head, and looked out at a window" (2 Kings 9:30).

It should be pointed out, first of all, that the portion of her face which she painted was the area around her *eyes.* The word here translated "face" *(Strong's Concordance,* #5869) is the common word for eyes. About 589 times it is translated "eye" or "eyes" in the Bible. The marginal rendering of this verse says: "...put her *eyes* in painting"; Goodspeed: "She painted her *eyelashes";* Moffatt: "...painting her *eyes";* Lamsa: "She painted her *eyelids* with kohl"; Rotherham: "She set her *eyes* in stibium"; Amplified: "She painted her *eyes";* etc. There is no doubt about it. The portion of the face that Jezebel painted was the area *around her eyes.*

Strangely enough, there are Christian women who use mascara on their eyes, but would not think of using lipstick on their lips—because Jezebel painted her face! They do not realize, apparently, that the specific part of the face that Jezebel painted was her eyes!

Jerusalem's unfaithfulness to God was sometimes likened to a woman who was unfaithful to her husband. The message of the prophets was that even though she made herself fair, her lovers would turn against her and she would be judged. In such a context the following verses were given:

"Ye have sent for men to come from far...and, lo, they came: for whom thou didst wash thyself, *paintedst thy eyes*, and deckedst thyself with ornaments" (Ezek. 23:40). And, "Though thou deckest thee with ornaments of gold, though thou rentest thy face [eyes][1] with painting, in vain shalt thou make thyself fair; thy lovers will despise thee, they will seek thy life" (Jer. 4:30).

These two verses, along with the one about Jezebel, have been quoted by those who oppose the use of makeup. However, the painting of the eyes was a common custom of the time. Other practices mentioned in these verses were equally common and unquestioned. In the case of Jezebel, we read that she "painted her face [eyes], and tired her hair, and looked out at a window." She "tired," that is, attired her hair. Some take this to mean that she combed her hair; others that she put on some type of hat. As far as we would know from this verse, if painting her eyes was a sin, then *so was combing her hair or putting on a hat!* Obviously, true doctrines or standards cannot be built on incidental statements such as these.

Before the woman mentioned in Ezekiel painted her eyes, she took a bath. Was this a sin? The woman mentioned in Jeremiah painted her eyes and clothed herself with crimson. But even the wearing of crimson, in itself, cannot have a bad meaning. The "virtuous woman" of Proverbs 31:21 clothed her household in scarlet (crimson).[2] Surely she was not clothing her household in an improper manner. David, in speaking of Saul's good points (2 Sam. 1:24), says that he clothed the daughters of Israel in scarlet (crimson).[2] The text in Jeremiah also mentions that this woman put on her ornaments. We have already seen that the use of ornaments was a common and unquestioned practice of women in the Bible.

Let us reason together. Luke tells about a woman with *long hair* whose sins were many (Lk. 7:37-47). Would this

---

[1] The word "face" in the text on Jezebel, the word "eyes" in Ezekiel 23:40, and the word "face" in Jeremiah 4:30 are all translated from *exactly the same word*, the common word for *eyes* (Strong's Concordance, #5869).

[2] "Scarlet" (*Strong's Concordance*, #8144) is the *same* word that is translated "crimson" in Jeremiah 4:30.

prove that all women who have long hair are sinners? Would the fact that Proverbs 7:17 mentions a harlot using perfume, prove that *all* women who use perfume are harlots? Or because an esteemed woman such as Esther was bathed and perfumed for one year (Esth. 2:12,13)—would this mean that women today should go to this extreme? Would the fact that an unfaithful wife wore jewelry (Hosea 2:13), prove that *all* women who wear jewelry are unfaithful? Of course not.

On the same basis, then, the fact that three scattered references to women painting their eyes (along with such things as taking a bath, fixing their hair, or putting on clothing) cannot prove that the use of cosmetics is wrong. It is the *motive*, the *attitude*, the *intention of the heart* that can make such "fixing up" right or wrong.

Women darkened their eyebrows, lashes, and the edges of the eyelids in order to make the white of the eyes look larger. *Clarke's Commentary* (Vol.4, p.35; Vol. 2, p.513) states: "This fashion seems to have prevailed very generally among the Eastern people in ancient times; and they retain the very same to this day....This staining of the eyes with stibium...was a universal custom."

JOB'S DAUGHTER

Job named one of his daughters Keren-happuch (Job 42:14), a name linked with the use of stibium on the eyes. *Dake's Annotated Reference Bible* points out that her name refers to a vessel made of horn, wherein Eastern women kept the paint used about their eyes to make them appear large and beautiful. *The Critical and Experimental Commentary* gives her name the meaning of "horn of stibium"; *Peloubet's Bible Dictionary* and the *Vulgate*, "Horn of Antimony"; the Masoretic text, "Horn of eye-paint"; *Young's Analytical Concordance*, "horn for paint"; and *Strong's Concordance* defines it as "horn of cosmetic."

I think the point is obvious. If the use of eye makeup was considered a bad practice, righteous Job would not have given this name to his daughter! Job's daughters were given names with *good* meanings. One was called Jemima, meaning fair as the day, a dove. The second, Kezia or Cassia, a highly cherished and fragrant spice of antiquity. The third,

Keren-happuch, a name linked with what was considered a sign of beauty—the painting of the eyes. All of Job's daughters no doubt used makeup on their eyes. Did this make them a disgrace to their father or did this make them look ugly by Bible standards? No. The Bible says: "In all the land were no women found so fair as the daughters of Job: and their father gave them inheritance among their brethren" (Job 42:15)!

In the scholarly work *Encyclopedia Judaica* (Vol. 5, p. 978), we read that "cosmetics, for the care and adornment of the body, were widely used by both men and women in the ancient Near East....Women used preparations to beautify the hair, to color eyelids, face, and lips....Women commonly put color around their eyes....Lips were colored with a cream made from oil combined with red ocher, and nails were painted with pigments mixed in ash or beeswax."

Camphire, mentioned in Song of Solomon (1:14; 4:13) and identified as henna *(Strong's Concordance,* #3724), provided a much used reddish-orange dye. Concerning this, the *Encyclopedia Judaica* (Vol. 9, p. 327) says: "Throughout the ages the peoples of the East prized this beautiful, fast dye which was used for dying the hair and nails." Henna was also used on the palms of the hands and soles of the feet.

Considering how well-known and how widely used these various forms of makeup were in the land of the Bible, if God was against such, why is it nowhere stated in the Bible? Out of the 31,101 verses in the Bible, not one gives a direct command against makeup.

Makeup has often been helpful in hiding blemishes and scars, and to improve the *natural* beauty. (Artificial beauty is not the point.) Dry skin, dull eyes, and pale lips have depressed many women and given them feelings of inferiority. The use of lipstick in hospitals has often proved to be a tonic in itself. Generally speaking, when a woman looks better, she feels better. Insisting that a woman must look dull does not cause her to have a cheerful mind or happy disposition.

Churches which have put too much emphasis on their doctrine of "no makeup" have caused a lot of undue misunderstanding. A woman, having come to Christ in one of these churches, may be told: "Now you are a Christian. You must take off you makeup and jewelry. You don't want to be like Jezebel who painted her face." As a result, she may lose all pride in her outward appearance, believing that the plainer she looks the more holy she is!

Her husband and children may tell her she would look better with some makeup. But she will not listen. She mistakenly believes God wants her to look dull. With the dull appearance often comes a dull personality. Some become so heavenly minded they are no earthly good.

Outings as a family are no longer encouraged in some cases. Since the world is so bad, why go anywhere or why see anything? But he who came to give abundant life does not require or even desire this negative outlook on life or the earth which he has given to the children of men.

Some churches will not allow a woman who wears makeup to sing in the choir. They figure this would be a bad example. If some preachers see a woman come into their church with lipstick on, they feel compelled to make their sermon a "salvation" message. How true is the statement: "Man looketh on the outward appearance, but the Lord looketh on the *heart*" (1 Sam. 16:7)!

DECORATION?

Some have opposed the use of makeup on the basis that it is *decoration.* But what is wrong with decoration? Wearing a dress with pretty colors might be considered decoration. Joseph had a coat of many colors. Was this wrong? The idea that any decoration is wrong has led to some foolish extremes. Some groups wear only dark clothing. In one such group, the people were told to paint the grills and bumpers of their cars black! Chrome, they reasoned, was too flashy for God.

We wonder where men ever got the idea that God wanted people to look drab. Nature is not this way. Suppose God had not included color in nature. Suppose the grass, trees, mountains, sunsets, lakes, and oceans were without color! Imagine orchids, lilies, violets, poppies, and roses without color! The garments of the high priest were bright and flashy.

The temple was decorated with gold. The "new Jerusalem" is described as having all sorts of dazzling stones and jewels.

We recognize, of course, that the use of bright colors in makeup and jewelry could easily be overdone and fail to convey a spirit of humility. But the extreme view that God requires a dull appearance (often accompanied with a dull personality) is certainly not consistent with the over-all teaching of the Bible. The very drabness can be made a display of vanity.

CHAPTER 4

SHOULD WOMEN WEAR
HEAD-COVERINGS?

There are within the epistles of Paul "some things *hard to be understood"* (2 Peter 3:16). Most commentators admit that 1 Corinthians 11:3-16 could be included in this category. It would appear that Paul was commanding the practice of veiling for women during worship, yet there is no other passage or example in the Bible to support this view. Besides, Paul's conclusion to this passage implies that *he had no such custom, neither the churches of God!*

Some feel that while veiling was not the Christian custom, yet because Corinth was a Greek city, Paul taught veiling for them because of *Greek* custom. But, as some commentators have pointed out, "the custom with Greeks of both sexes was to offer sacrifice *bareheaded."* So it does not seem likely that the veiling of women in worship stemmed from an old Greek custom.

Some teach that honorable women wore veils, but harlots went with their heads unveiled at Corinth. If this was the custom, and Paul was teaching veiling in view of this, one still wonders why he would speak specifically about veiling *within the assembly*—and that in connection with praying and prophesying. What about other times—and especially outside the assembly—if his concern was about a proper appearance before those outside the Christian faith? While it is possible that veiling was linked to some local custom, the passage itself speaks of such "because of the angels"!—a verse which has resulted in a great variety of explanations, none of which are entirely satisfactory.

Elsewhere Paul says there is *no difference* between men and women in Christ—in a spiritual sense. Was he in this case making a difference—requiring women to veil for worship? In another letter to the Corinthians, he speaks of the

29

veil being taken away in Christ. Though he was speaking of a *spiritual* veil being removed, this appears somewhat out of place if the women at Corinth still had to worship hidden behind a *literal* veil.

Still other difficulties appear in this passage. If Paul's question about men's hair means that it is a shame for a man to have long hair—how can we explain the fact that Paul himself (as we shall see) had long hair while at Corinth? There is not so much as a hint elsewhere in the Bible that long hair was a shame. To the contrary, there were many men in the Bible who had long hair. No wonder commentators speak of this passage as "difficult"!

We shall take a closer look at all of these questions, but for now, we should determine *what kind of veil* is being discussed in 1 Corinthians 11. Some assume that Paul was speaking of hats, scarves, doilies, or the like—just anything to cover the top (or part of the top) of the head. But the veil mentioned here covered not only the top of the head, *it hung clear down over the face as well!* The Greek word is *katakalupto* (*Strong's Concordance*, #2619). The prefix *kata* indicates the idea of "down"; *kalupto* has the meaning of "to cover wholly, to conceal." *Katakalupto* appears in the following places:

"...if a woman be not *covered*" (verse 6).

"...let her be *covered*" (verse 6).

"...a man ought not to *cover* his head" (verse 7).

In its noun form, the word translated "covered" is *kaluma*. Bullinger defines it as "a covering...a veil hiding all the face except the eyes and falling upon the shoulders." Liddell and Scott define it as "a covering, a hood or veil, a grave"; that is, the *kaluma* covered the whole head, even as a grave covers the whole body. That the *kaluma* covered the face (and not just the top of

30

the head) is clearly seen in the example of Moses who "put a veil [kaluma] over his face" (2 Cor. 3:13). It so completely covered his face that the brightness of his countenance could not be seen.

Now was Paul really commanding women to wear veils? Who does it today? What purpose could it serve? Realizing that such veiling could add nothing to true worship, and seeking to harmonize these words with the rest of the Bible, some believe that a portion of 1 Corinthians 11, possibly verses 4-10 about veiling, *may not be the words of Paul at all.* Instead, he may have been *quoting* from a letter he had received from the church elders at Corinth. This view may seem a little awkward at first. However, we do know that Paul had received a letter from the Corinthian church (1 Cor. 7:1). It is evident that much of this epistle was written in answer to questions which had been sent to him from this church.

We know also that in the Greek there were no quotation marks, questions marks, or any punctuation as we know it now. An example of Greek writing (taken from 1 Corinthians 11) is seen in the accompanying illustration. As far as we would know from the Greek text, verse 5 might just as well read: "Does every woman who prays or prophecies with her head uncovered dishonor her head?"—a *question.* Or, if written like a statement, but placed within quotation marks, it would indicate that Paul was *quoting* from the letter he had received. If Paul did refer to this letter in 1 Corinthians 11, the Corinthians —at the time— would have recognized the references to their letter. But now, almost 2,000 years later, we may not know exactly which statements were made by Paul and which might have been quotations from the letter he had received. It is possible, then, that a portion of this chapter —verses 4-10—referred to the elders' letter and was not the doctrine of Paul who had "no such custom." Bearing these things in mind, this view which is *possible* may even appear *probable* when we find that much of what is stated in these verses is contrary to EVERY OTHER VERSE IN THE BIBLE on the subjects covered!

In 1 Corinthians 11:4,7, for example, we read: "Every man praying or prophesying, having his head covered, dishonoreth his head...a man indeed ought not to cover his head." But there is nothing else in the Bible which would indicate this was wrong. To the contrary, the high priest in the Old Testament was to have his head covered as he ministered! "And he that is the high priest among his brethren...shall NOT UNCOVER HIS HEAD" (Lev. 21:10). Aaron and his sons all wore some type of headdress during their sacrificial rituals (Lev. 8:9,13; 10:6).

It was not wrong for Ezekiel to prophesy with something on his head. "The word of the Lord came unto me, saying...bind the tire of thine head upon thee, and put on thy shoes upon thy feet." After doing "these things," he began to prophesy: "Thus saith the Lord..." (Ezek. 24:15-21).

When Moses came down from mount Sinai his face shone and "he gave them in commandment all that the Lord had spoken with him in mount Sinai. And till Moses had done speaking with them, he put a vail on his face" (Ex. 34:32,33). *It was not wrong for Moses to prophesy with his head covered!*

Elijah "wrapped his face in his mantle" (1 Kings 19:13) as he stood in the presence of the Lord and spoke with him. When David fled from Absalom, he "went up by the ascent of mount Olivet, and wept as he went up, and had his HEAD COVERED...and all the people that was with him covered every man his head...and David said, O Lord, I PRAY thee, turn the counsel of Ahithophel into foolishness..." (2 Sam. 15:30-32). *It was not wrong for David or Elijah to pray with their heads covered!*

As the men of Jerusalem and Judah "covered their heads" (Jer. 14:3), modern Jews at prayer cover their heads with a tallith shawl—or, if not available, at least a skullcap as a sign of reverence. They consider praying bareheaded to be disgraceful—not the other way around.

WOMEN MUST PRAY WITH HEAD COVERED?

"Every woman that prayeth or prophesieth with her head uncovered dishonoreth her head" (1 Cor. 11:5). If this phrase is a statement of Paul (rather than a quotation from the letter), it would be saying that it is wrong for a woman to pray without a veil over her head. But why? Nowhere else in the Bible is there any command or example showing that a woman should veil when she prays. Hannah did not have a veil over her face when she prayed. Eli the priest noticed "her mouth...only her lips moved, but her voice was not heard" (1 Sam. 1:12,13). *Hannah was not doing wrong when she prayed without a veil.* Instead, her prayer was honored and answered!

Many have seen pictures of Arab women with the hideous face-veils and assume that such were commonly worn by women in Bible times. But the use of such veils dates from the spread of the *Koran* which forbids women to appear with heads unveiled before any but their nearest relatives. Such is an *Islamic* custom, not a Christian custom.

In the Bible, there is only an *occasional* mention of the use of a veil. Rebekah "took a veil and covered herself." *If* this was a *face*-veil, its use had significance only because she was about to meet the man who would become her husband. Prior to this, she did not have a veil on, as when she talked to Abraham's servant (Gen. 24:65). Judah supposed that a certain woman who "covered her face" with a veil was a harlot (Gen. 38:14,15), a fact which indicates that women *in general* did not wear a veil covering their face. (References to veils in Ruth 3:15, Song of Solomon 5:7, and Isaiah 3:23—translated from different words—refer to forms of clothing not directly linked with covering the face.)

There is nothing to imply that *face* veils were a common article of clothing for women of the Bible. Sarah did not wear a veil over her face, for "when Abraham was come into Egypt, the Egyptians beheld the woman that she was very fair" (Gen. 12:14). When Jacob saw Rachel, he kissed her. She had no veil over her face (Gen. 29:10,11). The clothing God provided for Eve did not include a veil. The fact that women in the Bible used jewelry such as *earrings*, *nose* rings, and jewels for the *forehead* also shows they did not go about with their heads hidden behind a veil. Paul's comment about a woman's braided hair (1 Tim. 2:9) could have little point—one way or another—if the hair was covered with a veil. The Bible mentions women such as Sarah, Rebekah, Miriam, Elizabeth, Mary, Martha, and many more. Never are we told that any of them put on a veil in order to pray!

Returning to 1 Corinthians 11, what were the reasons given as to why a woman should veil and a man should not? Verses 4 and 5 say that if a man veils when he prays, he *dishonors his head;* but if a woman does not veil, she *dishonors her head.* But what kind of reasoning is this? Just before, Paul said he wanted them to know that the head of every man is Christ, the head of the woman is the man, and the head of Christ is God (verse 3). The fact that the man has a head, and not the woman only, actually destroys the theory that a woman must veil because *she* has a head. Does Christ have to veil because he has a head? No. Does the man have to veil because he has a head? No. Why, then, would a woman have to veil because she has a head?

The word translated "head" throughout this portion is the same, whether referring to a head (as a leader) or to the literal heads of men and women. In the Greek there may have been a play on words; that is, the true headship compared with some useless custom about whether one must veil his or her physical head.

A "reason" given in verse 7 as to why a man should not cover his head is because "he is the image and glory of God: but the woman is the glory of the man." What can this mean? If a woman must wear a veil because she is the glory of the man, then the man, being the glory of God, would have to wear a veil too! In no other passage in the Bible are we told that man is the image and glory of God, but the woman is not. All believers are "conformed to the image of his Son"

(Rom. 8:29; Col. 3:10). All of us "with open face" are changed into the *same image* from glory to glory (2 Cor. 3:18). Both men and women are changed into the same image and reflect the glory of the Lord. Why, then, should we suppose Paul would say that the man is the glory and image of God, but the woman is not?

BECAUSE OF THE ANGELS?

Then in verse 10 we read: "For this cause ought the woman to have *power* on her head *because of the angels.*" We might question what this wording "power on her head" can mean. Translators commonly *add* a few words here, as in the marginal rendering: "that is, a covering, in sign that she is under the power of her husband." But as far as the scriptures are concerned, there is no proof that a veil is a sign of subjection. If it did symbolize subjection, then why wouldn't a man wear one too, since he is said to be subject to Christ?

The idea that a woman must veil *"because of the angels"* has resulted in a long list of guesses by expositors as to its proper meaning—none being very satisfactory. Strangely enough, some feel that if a woman prayed or prophesied with her head uncovered, the very sight of her *hair* might have caused angels to be tempted to lust! This belief may stem from an idea held by some rabbis—that angels (Gen. 6) once got possession of women by their hair. We can only say that if angels are in danger of being led into lust because they see a woman's face or her hair in a church meeting, their moral stability is very weak. If this is the case, why the mention of when women are praying or prophesying? What about other times? There are a number of verses in the Bible in which angels talked to women, but in no reference are we told that these women put veils on their heads (Judges 13:3,9; Lk. 1:28; etc.).

Taking everything into consideration, the idea that women should veil "because of the angels" sounds more like an oral tradition the elders at Corinth had mistakenly adopted, rather than a teaching of Paul. As to Paul's doctrine, consider what he wrote in another letter to the church at Corinth. After speaking of "Moses, which put a veil over his face," Paul said that those who follow Moses (instead of

Christ), have a veil over them in the reading of the Old Testament. "BUT WE"—notice the contrast! "But we ALL"—men and women who have turned to the Lord through the gospel—"WITH OPEN FACE" (not with a veil over it!) "beholding as in a glass the glory of the Lord, are changed into the same image from glory to glory" (2 Cor. 3:3-18). The point is that the veil is removed through Christ—spiritually speaking. But would there be any point if the veil was removed *spiritually*, yet women had to wear a veil *literally?* If Paul had actually commanded veiling in First Corinthians, these words in Second Corinthians would be difficult indeed to understand.

COMPARING SCRIPTURE WITH SCRIPTURE

We see, then, that a number of statements in verses 4-10 simply do not fit with other verses in the Bible. Instead of it being a dishonor for a man to pray with something on his head, we have Biblical examples in which men did pray in this way. Nowhere else are we told that women must veil for prayer. There is no support for the idea that man is the image and glory of God, but the woman is not. The idea that women must veil because of the angels is without any supporting scripture. Then verses 8 and 9 say: "For the man is not of the woman; but the woman of the man. Neither was the man created for the woman; but the woman for the man." Biblically speaking, the woman was originally created for the man. But even this statement must be qualified. This Paul does in verses 11 and 12: "Nevertheless"—note the contrast that comes in now—"neither is the man without the woman, neither the woman without the man, in the Lord. For as the woman is of the man, *even so, is the man also by the woman;* but all things of *God."*

Paul is saying that even in the natural creation, the woman is of the man and the man of the woman. It takes both a man and a woman to produce another life. But, when all is said and done, all life stems from God anyhow—"all things of God." Furthermore, *spiritually speaking,* "there is neither male or female: for ye are all one in Christ Jesus" (Gal. 3:28). Why, then, in spiritual things—such as praying and prophesying—should women (and not men) have to be veiled?

Next, Paul appeals to their own power of *reason,* verse 13: "Judge in yourselves: is it comely that a woman pray unto God uncovered?"—without the *kaluma* veil. Even their own judgment should indicate that it was not uncomely for a woman to pray without the veil. Hannah had no veil on when she prayed—nor is there any record of any other woman in the Bible who prayed while veiled! As far as the original text is concerned, verse 13 could just as well have been translated: "Judge in yourselves: it is comely that a woman pray unto God without the veil."

I have been in homes of people who believe women must always have something on their heads before they can pray. If prayer is to be offered over food or before leaving the home, each woman or girl must quickly look around the house to find a towel, a scarf, a handkerchief—something to put on her head so prayer can be offered! But such adds neither power nor virtue to prayer.

A MAN'S LONG HAIR

Next Paul appeals to an argument from *nature.* What the KJV translators give as a question—"Doth not even nature itself teach you, that, if a man have long hair, it is a shame unto him?"—could just as correctly be translated: "Even nature does not teach you, that, if a man have long hair, it is a shame unto him."[1]

What, then, was Paul saying? That nature teaches it is a shame for a man to have long hair? Or was he saying nature does not make this distinction?

Speaking strictly from the viewpoint of *nature,* both the hair of men *and* women will grow long if not cut. In fact, the record for the longest hair of all time has been claimed—not by a woman—but by a *man.* An Indian monk, Swami Pandarasannadhi, was reported in 1949 as having hair 26 feet long! *(Guinness Book of World Records,* p. 38).

---

[1] The words "doth not even" are used to translate *one word* in the Greek: *oude (Strong's Concordance,* #3761). It occurs 134 times in the New Testament—translated "neither" 68 times; "nor" 31 times; "not" 10 times; "no not" 8 times; and in the 17 remaining references by 12 different words of similar meaning. In the Greek, this verse simply says: "NEITHER does nature teach you..." or "Even nature DOES NOT teach you..."

Since Corinth was a Greek city, we might well ask: Did nature teach the people of Corinth, as *Greeks*, that long hair was a shame for a man? To the contrary, in ancient times at least, "ancient Greek men wore hair so long they had to braid it in topknots on the crowns of their heads and hold it in place with hairpins" *(The Long and Short of It—5,000 Years of Fun and Fury Over Hair*, p. 24).

Greek men were noted for their long hair as seen in Homer's numerous references to them as the "long-haired Greeks." Later, shorter hair styles for men did come into acceptance, but not without suspicion on the part of some. There were those who felt short hair for men was a sign of effeminate weakness and that such would undermine the strength of the nation! In Corinth, Diogenes walked the streets shining a lantern into the faces of those he passed looking for an honest man. He wanted one with long hair—as he thought any real man should wear! It is apparent, then, that at earlier times long hair for a man was not considered a shame by the Greeks—short hair was. Is it possible by the time Paul wrote that their feelings about long hair for men had completely reversed, so that now long hair was considered a shame instead of short hair? It is possible, but it does not seem conclusive.

Did those at Corinth with a *Jewish* background (for the converts at Corinth were from among the Jews and the Greeks—Acts 18:4) hold the belief that long hair was a shame for a man? Or did they, *as Christians*, hold this belief? Apparently not, for the scriptures (which made up their Bible) give many examples of men who had long hair—some even at the command of God!

It was not considered a shame for Absalom to have long hair. "But in all Israel there was none to be so much praised as Absalom for his beauty...and when he polled his head, (for it was at every year's end that he polled it: because the hair was heavy on him, therefore he polled it:) he weighed the hair of his head at two hundred shekels after the king's weight" (2 Sam. 14:25,26). That Absalom had "long hair" cannot be disputed. We notice also that it was not cut because of a divine commandment against long hair, but because it became too heavy.

38

It has sometimes been debated whether Jesus had long hair. Artists have commonly painted him thus. The Bible itself does not tell us his hair was long, nor does it tell us it was short. It simply does not say.

Some might assume that from Adam on down through Biblical history that most men had short hair. There is no foundation for this whatsoever. In those primitive times, men like Noah, Abraham, Isaac, Jacob, Moses, etc., probably had hair that many today would consider "long." Without the sophisticated hair cutting equipment that is now available, we can be sure that they were not able to have the finely trimmed sideburns or the neatly clipped exposure of the ear that is now common. In most cases, the hair probably hung down over the ears. Jonathan told David: "My father will do nothing either great or small, but that he will shew it me," or, as the margin says: "uncover my ear" (1 Sam. 20:2, 12; 22:8,17). This wording, as Biblical commentators point out, probably referred to one telling a closely guarded secret at close range to the other person. In so doing, he would uncover the hair from the ear and whisper the message to him.

If it was a shame for a man to have long hair, why was this one of the requirements for Nazarites—men who were especially dedicated to God? (Num. 6:2-5). Would something that was a "shame" be a proper symbol of Nazarites? Nazarites were to abstain from "wine and strong drink" (verse 3). Concerning John the baptist, an angel said: "He shall be great in the sight of the Lord, and shall drink neither wine nor strong drink" (Lk. 1:15). The similarity between these two verses seems so close, it is highly possible that John may have been a Nazarite and, as such, would have had long hair.

A very famous example of a Nazarite was, of course, Samson. An angel told his mother: "No rasor shall come on his head: for the child shall be a Nazarite unto God" (Judges 13:5). Nature did not stop Samson's hair from growing. It was so long, in fact, that Delilah could weave his seven locks on a hand-loom! (Judges 16:13,14). In the story of Samson, his sin was not having long hair; it was when his hair was cut off that the Lord departed from him (verses 17-20).

Samuel also had long hair. Hannah prayed: "I will give him unto the Lord all the days of his life, and there shall no rasor come upon his head" (1 Sam. 1:11).

Unlike Samson and Samuel, however, not all Nazarites were Nazarites for life. Instead the laws regarding Nazarites had to do with a vow taken for a period of time. "All the days of the *vow*...there shall no rasor come upon his head: UNTIL the days be fulfilled" (Num. 6:5). There were in the church at Jerusalem four Jewish men which had taken a vow. During the time of their vow they let their hair grow long, after which it was shaved off and they purified themselves (Acts 21:23-27). We see, then, that the practice of letting the hair grow long during the time of a vow was apparently still a custom at that time. For these men to have long hair was not considered a shame!

Following this same custom, *Paul himself* had allowed his hair to grow long during the time of a vow, after which he cut his hair off. Thus we read in Acts 18:18 that Paul sailed into Syria, "having SHORN HIS HEAD in Cenchrea: for he had a VOW." Now an ordinary haircut would not be anything significant to record. Instead, this was clearly a case of his hair being sheared off following the period of a vow, during which it had grown long.

This point seems especially significant in connection with our study of 1 Corinthians 11, for it was during Paul's extended stay AT CORINTH (Acts 18) that he did not cut his hair! When he left Corinth his hair was still not cut. It was not cut until he got to Cenchrea, the eastern seaport of Corinth, where he boarded a ship to continue his missionary journey! Doesn't it seem strange that Paul would write to the Corinthians and tell them it is a shame for a man to have long hair *when he, himself, had long hair while at Corinth?*

In view of all these things we have mentioned, it is very possible that Paul's words should be understood as a statement: "Nature does not teach it is a shame for a man to have long hair." If so, then verse 15—which is connected in the line of thought—is saying that neither does nature teach that if a woman have long hair it is her glory! That is, hair could not be, by nature, a woman's glory exclusively, for a man's hair will grow long too. All of this would actually argue against the artificial distinction which would teach that a woman must veil and a man must not.

Let me hasten to say, parenthetically, that I do not mean to imply that I think men should grow long hair! This is not the point. The proper length of a man's hair might be determined more by the customs at a given time or place. Whether some of us personally care for a long hair style on men or not, we cannot correctly say there is any direct Biblical command against it. Even if nature in some way did teach the people at Corinth that long hair was a shame, Paul's reference to what nature taught *them* could hardly be a basis of doctrine for us. The evidence would only be indirect at best. In view of this, I think it is sad that some churches have made the length of a man's hair—or the length of his sideburns or how his hair should be combed—a major point of doctrine and division. The real objectives of Christianity are far above fighting and dividing over such things.

If Paul was not commanding veiling (assuming a portion of this passage was a reference to the letter he had received), then we can understand his conclusion: "We have no such custom, neither the churches of God." Or, if he had no such custom, but taught veiling at Corinth because of a local situation there—*either way*, it seems clear that this passage can hardly be a command for Christian women to wear *kaluma* veils. On this, I think there must be agreement, for we do not see women wearing such veils in churches today.

A passage with difficulties of interpretation—regardless of which view we favor—is not a sound basis on which to build dogmatic rules. In the interpretation of the Bible, the clear portions must explain the unclear—not the other way around. It is also considered a sound rule of interpretation that "in the mouth of two or three witnesses shall every word be established" (2 Cor. 13:1; Matt. 18:16). All essential doctrines are based on two or more scriptures. But this portion presents things about veils and hair that are *unsupported* by other verses, and, in some instances, are *contrary* to other verses. Bearing this in mind, we feel that the view we have presented has definite merit. Nevertheless, we present it "as a study," certainly not as a dogmatic or infallible conclusion.

CHAPTER 5

SHOULD WOMEN CUT THEIR HAIR?

Don't ever bob your hair girls, it's an awful sin;
If you ever bob your hair girls, you'll never enter in.

These are the words of a little chorus a man I know used
to sing as a special number in church. They reflect a view,
held by some, that a Christian woman must *never* cut her
hair. A woman's hair is not to be touched by scissors, they
reason, for it is "a shame for a woman to be shorn or shaven"
(1 Cor. 11:6). Those who hold this view seem to think that
"shorn" means any cutting of the hair. This is not the case.
"Shorn" is simply the past participle of the word *shear*. If a
woman has her head shaved or shorn, the hair is removed
right down to the scalp!

There were at Corinth certain cult prostitutes who had
shaved heads—though, as Lenski points out, "only a few of
the very lowest type had shaved heads" *(Commentary on
First Corinthians*, p. 439). Because of this, we can understand why a woman's shaved head was a sign of "shame" at
Corinth—and thus the reference in 1 Corinthians 11:6. But
what does any of this have to do with a Christian woman
today merely having her hair *cut?* There is no connection
whatsoever.

While the shaved head was considered a shame at
Corinth—because of its association with harlotry—it was
not necessarily a sign of shame elsewhere. Instead, shaving
off the hair of the head—as strange as this practice would
appear to us today!—was *a common sign of mourning.* In the
scriptures, there are numerous references to people making
themselves bald by shearing or shaving off the hair of their
heads.

Job shaved his head and mourned (Job 1:20; 2:11,13).
Other verses include the following: "They shall make them-

selves utterly bald...they shall weep" (Ezek. 27:31). "Make thee bald, and poll thee for thy delicate children...for they are gone into captivity" (Micah 1:16). "...all of them mourning...and baldness upon every head" (Amos 8:10). "On all their heads shall be baldness...weeping abundantly" (Isaiah 15:2; also Jer. 16:6; 48:37; Isaiah 22:12; Ezra 9:3; etc.).

Both men and women shaved off their heads in times of extreme mourning—not just men. Troubles that were to come upon Jerusalem would cause the daughters of Zion to mourn and put on sackcloth. Instead of well set hair, they would have *baldness*—the result of hair being shaved off in mourning (Isaiah 3:24). Jerusalem, likened to a woman, was told: "Cut off thine hair, O Jerusalem, and cast it away, and take up a lamentation" (Jer. 7:29).

If a soldier of Israel took a wife from among the captives of war, the instructions were that "she shall shave her head," mourn for her parents for one month, and then become his wife (Deut. 21:10-14). If it is a sin for a woman to cut her hair—as some suppose—how can we explain the instructions here in which a woman's hair was not just cut, but even shaved off? If it was not a sin in the Bible for a woman to shave off all the hair of her head in a time of mourning—as the custom then was—how can it be a sin for a Christian woman today to merely have part of her hair cut off?

Churches which make legalistic rules about women's hair have caused unnecessary confusion and unhappiness. While they pride themselves in having a high standard, they sometimes become judges—judging by the outward appearance. A Christian lady I know visited a church which does not allow women to cut their hair. Her hair was a normal length for a woman—but not the length required by this church. The minister called on the congregation for testimonies, asking all who were going to testify to stand up. Finally it got back to where this lady was standing, waiting her turn. Then the preacher, sounding somewhat hostile, said: "I don't allow women with short hair to testify in MY church!" She was told to sit down.

At different times, a number of women from this same church had gone to a Christian doctor asking what they could do for headaches. In several cases the doctor felt the weight of their uncut hair piled on their heads was a contributing factor to their problem. But the "hair" thing was so big in their church, they could not cut part of it off!

We have seen women who give others the impression that they are especially "holy" because they have long, uncut hair. They feel they are given this long hair for a *covering!* Yet what does it cover? It is commonly worn on top of their heads instead of hanging down. It neither covers their face, back, or neck. It covers little more than the short hair on a man's head.

Some insist that a woman is to have "long hair" which (to them) means hair that is not cut or trimmed by scissors. Yet if they see a man with hair that hangs down to his shoulders—*even though a few inches have been cut off by scissors*—they smoothly change their definition and say he is a shame because he has "long hair."

If the explanation we gave earlier is correct, that "even nature itself does not teach you, that, if a man have long hair, it is a shame unto him," then the second part of the statement would read: "[Nor does nature teach] if a woman have long hair, it is a glory to her: for her hair is given her for a *covering*" (1 Corinthians 11:14,15). The word "covering" here is not the same Greek word that was used earlier in this chapter. Here it is *peribolaion (Strong's Concordance,* #4018), which means "something thrown around one." In the one other place it appears, it is translated "vesture" (Heb. 1:12). It means simply *clothing.* The line of thought connects verses 14 and 15 together. The point is, according to "nature" a man's long hair is not a *shame;* nor is a woman's long hair her *glory*—as though it were given to her *for clothing* (or literally, instead of clothing)!

On the other hand, if we are to understand this passage about what "nature" teaches as a rule that women must have long hair, this is still not the extreme view that the hair can *never* be cut. "Long hair" does not, necessarily, mean hair that is never cut or trimmed. Furthermore, if a woman had to have hair hanging down her back in order to be a Christian, *millions* of women would be automatically excluded. *Women of some races simply do not have hair that grows long!*

We are not instructed to take a measuring tape to see if a woman's hair is long enough to qualify her for church membership! Instead, the Christian woman is left at liberty to wear her hair the length she finds comfortable, practical and appropriate within the realm of her own Christian convictions.

WHAT ABOUT BEARDS?

While it may be true that most women in the Bible wore their hair in a long style, there is no direct Biblical commandment for so doing. There would actually be more Biblical support for men wearing *beards*, than for the idea that a woman must never trim her hair. Yet, the vast majority of those men who insist on uncut hair for women, do not, themselves, wear a beard!

For a moment, consider a few things about beards. Men in the Bible such as Aaron (Psalms 133:2), Mephibosheth (2 Sam. 19:24), David (1 Sam. 21:13), Ezra (Ezra 9:3), and Ezekiel (Ezek. 5:1) are all specifically mentioned as having beards. A verse, commonly applied to the sufferings of Jesus, indicates that he had a beard: "I gave my back to the smiters, and my cheeks to them that plucked off the hair" (Isaiah 50:6). The apostles apparently also had beards, for Jesus and his apostles looked enough alike that Judas had to point out which one was Jesus (Matt. 26:48).

All of David's servants had beards. We read that Hanun, supposing them to be spies, "took David's servants, and shaved off the one half of their beards, and cut off their garments in the middle, even to their buttocks, and sent them away" (2 Sam. 10:4). Even though their *garments* were cut off, they seem to have been especially embarrassed because of what happened to their *beards!* "The men were greatly ashamed"; so David told them to stay at Jericho "until your beards be grown, and then return"!

Since boys before reaching the age of manhood, and also eunuchs, were without facial hair, primitive man reasoned that a beard was not only an indication of male virility, some believed it was the very source of it! But for whatever reasons men in the Bible wore beards, they did so because of custom, not divine commandment.

45

That the wearing of beards was not an inflexible command is seen by the fact that Joseph "shaved himself" (Gen. 41:14) when he was taken from the dungeon to appear before Pharaoh. Since the Egyptians did not wear beards, it seems probable that Joseph followed the Egyptian custom in order to appear acceptable before Pharaoh. On this same basis, whether a man wants a beard or not is entirely up to him as an individual. The Bible does not command it.

We believe it is proper for a woman to look like a woman and a man like a man in matters of dress and appearance —according to time and place. However, this rule must have its necessary limitations, otherwise a beard would be an *absolute requirement* for all men. A beard *clearly* identifies the face of a man from that of a woman. It is also true that among people who normally wore beards, when some men began to shave, they were accused of trying to look like women! In view of these things, it is not very consistent for *men* to accuse women of trying to look like men (because they wear slacks or have their hair cut) when these men shave off their beards.

CHAPTER 6

WOMEN'S MODEST APPAREL

Though it may sound strange to say, the Bible does not give an inflexible or uniform clothing code. It does not specify any certain *color*—people in the Bible wore clothing of different colors. As to *style*, various robe-type garments were worn, but no certain style of clothing is commanded. As to *material*, originally God made "coats of skins" to cloth Adam and Eve, but this did not mean all people from then on must wear only leather! Garments made from different materials are mentioned in the Bible.

We are told, however, that women should "adorn themselves in *modest* apparel" (1 Tim. 2:9). What, then, is modest apparel? Does this mean, as some have taught, that a woman cannot wear short sleeves? How long must a woman's skirt be? Where does modesty begin or end? One inch below the knee or an inch above?

Some churches make rules about the length of a woman's skirt. One church set a certain number of inches above the floor as a maximum. It didn't seem to matter that some women were shorter, some taller than others! All skirts had to come within the given number of inches from the floor! In all cases, the skirt was long enough to completely cover the knees—this being their major objective.

As to sleeves, some believe a woman must always wear long sleeves so that her *elbows* are covered. But are exposed elbows really so erotically stimulating that men might be tempted? I have lived in areas where the summers are hot. I have seen women with their long sleeves, suffering from the heat. They must keep those elbows covered! There they are, having their pie and cake sales on the shopping center sidewalk to raise money for their church! (Even the priests were not required to wear garments which would make them sweat: "They shall not gird themselves with anything that causeth sweat"—Ezekiel 44:18). I have wondered why those who insist that knees and elbows must be covered at all times do not require a *face* covering also. After all, would not a pretty face be more attractive than a pair of knees or elbows?

Do not misunderstand. I believe in standards of decency. When many have no values or convictions, we admire people who try to hold a high standard. But when big issues are made about non-essential points—when some would major on minors—people are driven to a legalism that hinders an effective Christian testimony.

IDEAS ABOUT MODESTY

Ideas about "modesty" have varied greatly in different countries. In old China, exposure of the upper-class women's tiny feet was regarded as most indecent. Such were considered the most sexually stimulating parts of the body. Virgin goddesses were sometimes portrayed with shoes, even when otherwise stark naked. In early Japan, a woman's eyebrows were considered as among her greatest charms. Some husbands would shave their brides' eyebrows off in an attempt to make them unattractive to other men. Among some people, a woman's hair was considered a sexual stimulant —that the mere sight of her hair aroused a man's passions. Thus it had to be covered.

In Islamic countries where women must cover their faces with veils, a woman's first reaction might be to cover her face, rather than her body, if suddenly surprised while unclothed. Among tribes that wear no clothing, embarrassment is experienced when one is made to *put on* clothing before others! Australian aboriginal women who normally go about naked, will put on feather skirts for certain indecent dances.

There are missionary magazines which have carried group pictures of native women in Africa, some with bare breasts—a custom completely unquestioned in many areas of the world—yet the same magazines would not think of printing such pictures had they been taken of women in this country. A foreign missionary might preach in short pants—in common with his audience in areas of extreme heat and humidity—yet in other places this would seem quite out of place.

What might be proper or practical clothing in Hawaii, would be impractical and out of place in Alaska. What one might wear to work in the yard would not generally be what he would wear to church. What one might wear to swim in would not be practical for shopping, etc. The legalist fails to admit that circumstances alter cases.

A skirt extending a few inches below the knees—which even most of the strict people would now approve—might have been considered improper during the last century when dresses extended almost to the ground. When the dresses were shortened slightly, it is said that some men became embarrassed at the sight of a woman's *ankle*. Later, when dresses were shortened even more—though the hem was still *below the knees*—some became alarmed. As one writer says: "The cry of Sodom and Gomorrah went up from every pulpit in the country" *(Muffs and Morals*, p.30).

I spoke once for a group that felt all their women should dress the way women did in about 1900, fix their hair by styles of that time, etc. This, to them, was the old-time religion. But by doing this, they were actually drawing *more attention* to the "outward man" than if they wore clothing similar to other women of the time. By dressing in clothing radically different than others, they defeated the very thing they supposed they were accomplishing. Even plain or out of date clothes can be worn with vanity—the very drabness or difference draws attention to the outward person, not the inner man.

HOW STRICT?

How *strict* must we be? Must we lock ourselves away in total silence—lest we speak a wrong word? There have been monks who have gone for years without uttering a word. Did this make them more holy? There have been men who have lived in monasteries or deserted places so they would not see the face of a woman. But did this make them immune to

49

lust? What about their minds? Many were like St. Jerome (fourth century) who confessed: "When I was living in the desert...how often did I fancy myself among the pleasures of Rome!...I often found myself amid bevies of girls. My face was pale and my frame chilled with fasting; yet my mind was burning with desire, and the fires of lust kept bubbling up." Some in an attempt to be holy even castrated themselves, one notable example being Origen.

St. Bessarion for forty years, St. Pachomius for fifty years, never laid down while sleeping. Macarius slept in a marsh for six months exposing his naked body to poisonous flies. In northern Syria, about 422 A.D., Simeon built a column 60 feet high, on the top of which he lived for 30 years exposed to rain, sun, and cold. In a convent of the fourth century, 130 nuns never bathed or washed their feet. Such was also the practice of St. Anthony and St. Clemet.

Some people carried heavy weights. St. Marcian restricted himself to one meal a day in order to be continually plagued with hunger. The morbid extremism in these examples is apparent.

Even in our time, some become so strict they are driven to foolish extremes. The Bible is against making an idol or image to bow down to it (Ex. 20:4,5). But some, completely misapplying this verse, will not allow their children to have a doll or stuffed toy. One group went so far as to say that a person should take all the labels off canned goods—that it was idolatry to have a can in the house with a picture of peaches (or whatever) on the can! They were against wall paper with flowers on it. They supposed these flowers were images!

Some will not have their picture taken. I know people who have destroyed all of their photographs, including irreplaceable family photos. One sect considers the mirror an invention of the devil. A person looking into it makes an image!

Some people are so opposed to the evils of alcohol that they will not use shaving lotion or flavorings that have an alcohol content. Since the Bible says not to drink blood, some believe it would be better to die than to take a blood transfusion. One woman was against soda pop because the Bible says not to use strong drink! There have been people who would not eat potatoes, because the word "potatoes" does not appear in the Bible! And in ways that are sometimes just as inconsistent, men have made a series of "don'ts" for women. Don't wear lipstick. Don't wear short sleeves. Don't trim your hair. Don't wear slacks. Don't wear jewelry.

Some feel that if a doctrine is not harsh and strict, it is not the "old-time religion." But a study of Acts 15 shows that the apostles were against imposing rules on the people that God has not placed on them. By this decision, they were not "lowering their standards" nor did it indicate any spiritual laxness on their part. Where, then, do we draw the line? On what basis should standards be measured?

I can only say that as Christians we should turn our eyes upon *Jesus.* The total attitude of Jesus—which was often in sharp contrast to the unfruitful strictness of the Pharisees —should be our example in forming Christian convictions.

The Pharisees, compared to the Sadducees, might have been considered the "holiness" branch of the Jewish religion. They were very strict about their tithing, fasting, rules, and regulations. They were known for their carefully washed hands, their long robes, and long prayers. Yet with all of this external religion, they missed the *true* program of God and failed to recognize Jesus as the Christ. They would bind "heavy burdens and grievous to be borne, and lay them on men's shoulders" (Matt. 23:4). In their zeal, they would "compass sea and land to make one proselyte" (verse 15).

Jesus spoke of them as "blind guides, which strain at a gnat [or literally, strain *out* a gnat], and swallow a camel" (Matt. 23:24). So strict were they for the letter of the law, they would strain their water or wine through linen gauze lest they swallow a tiny insect. Yet, figuratively, they would swallow a camel.

The inconsistency to which their strictness led them is well illustrated by the woman they brought to Jesus who had committed adultery. They claimed she had been caught "in the very act." They argued that Moses had said she should be stoned. They had *"Bible"* for their argument. *Yet they failed to see their own attitude was wrong.* In committing adultery, it is evident a *man* was involved, but nothing whatsoever was said about the man! It was the *woman* they frowned upon and would have stoned! Besides, how did they catch her in the very act? Were they snooping around trying to find someone to accuse?

The answer of Jesus was that anyone without sin could cast the first stone. When there were no accusers, Jesus said, "Neither do I condemn thee: go, and sin no more" (John 8:3-11). "For God sent not his Son into the world to *condemn* the world; but that the world through him might be *saved*" (John 3:17).

How shocked those Pharisee leaders must have been when Jesus said: "The *harlots* go into the kingdom before you" (Matt. 21:31). But repentance comes easier to sinners than to self-righteous people who feel they have no need of repentance.

Such is seen in the case of the woman with whom Jesus talked at the well of Samaria. She had been married five times and was now living with a man to whom she was not married. For Jesus to talk to this woman was contrary to the religious dogmas of the day. How did it look for a preacher to be talking to a woman of questionable character? Rabbis were not to converse with women in public or instruct them in the law. A rabbi was not to even converse with his wife, sister, or daughter in public or in the street! Besides, she was a Samaritan, and Jews—because of another uninspired dogma—had no dealings with Samaritans. No wonder the disciples "marvelled that he talked with the woman" (John 4:7-27)! But Jesus was more concerned about the needs of the individual than religious rules made by people who suppose *law* is greater than *love*.

Considering the *relative* nature of modesty, seeing the inconsistency to which a *strict over-emphasis* on non-essential points has led, and weighing all of this in the light of *the total spirit and example of Jesus*, I think that certain conclusions are apparent. The wisdom of a *balanced* view seems clear. We should avoid the *extremes*, seeking rather the CENTER of God's will. We need not wear rags to be holy, nor do we need to have the most expensive clothes money can buy. It is possible for a person through the use of makeup, jewelry, or some forms of clothing to appear too flashy. But the other extreme, a dull and drab appearance, is not a requirement for the victorious Christian.

Clothes can be worn too tight—and draw attention. By the same token, the continual wearing of baggy clothes can also be made a display. The balanced Christian view—of all the things we have mentioned in this book—seems clearly to be that we should dress according to the custom of our time and country, with a sense of decency and wisdom.

Let us take a stand for the high standards of the gospel; let us stand firm for honesty, fairness, kindness, integrity, and love; let us practice holiness, but let it be "*true* holiness" from the heart, not a false holiness as that of the Pharisees. Let us never confuse the over-all objectives of Christianity with petty points of men's traditions, remembering that "the kingdom of God is not meat and drink; but righteousness, and peace, and joy in the Holy Ghost" (Rom. 14:17). In essentials, then, let there be *unity;* in non-essentials, *liberty;* and in all things, *charity.*

LETTERS

I am most grateful to my Lord for placing the book *Women's Adornment* into my hands. What a blessing to my heart it has been...—Montana.

Your book...is not only a very interesting book, but one which I feel is the most comprehensive and scriptural approach that I have read on the subject. This particular subject has caused considerable amount of division and difficulty....Thank you very much for your good book. —(pastor) Arizona.

I am writing because you need to hear the good report about your book on the adornment of God's women. You can not even imagine how that book has stirred so many....My copy is getting worn already....I've had people tell me, "You're so worldly wearing earrings," etc.—all sorts of insulting things....For years as a child I heard over and over again about what a woman should *not* wear....God bless you for being a willing vessel to be used of God. —New York.

When I read you book it set me free from the bondage of legalism. Praise God! A preacher with a church of around 3,000 read your book in 1981...it set him free from legalism....Thank God for you and for the truth. —Texas

"Thank you" is not enough to tell you how much your book has meant to me....In the past, my outward dress was stressed so much and constantly preached about that other things were just overlooked. My husband and I had questions and our pastor could not or would not answer them. Someone told us about your book during our search for the truth. Thank you, thank you, thank you. Such a load has been lifted. I can serve the Lord out of love now, instead of fear. I am ordering more of your books in hope that I can help someone else before they go into a state of depression like we did before we found you... —Illinois.

Many thanks for the paperback *Women's Adornment*. I have been lending it out to interested Bible students....It is most interesting and enlightening. My friends are delighted.—(minister/author) England.

I read your book "Women's Adornment." I would like to thank you for taking the time to study the scriptures and to put it all down in a book. I just wish I had come upon this book years ago. The book I read was someone else's and I am interested in purchasing several so I can pass them on to other people that would appreciate this book....Please send information on cost of the book (at least a dozen) maybe more....I am very anxious to get these books.—Florida.

A woman sent me what you had printed up about women wearing pants or slacks....Women who wear these are an abomination to the Lord....I don't need junk by modern man to tell me how to dress. The Bible is good enough for me, old King James that is, and not any modern new ones....As long as we got preachers with itching ears, hell will continue to enlarge itself....Hope you wake up fellow. I can always be thankful I don't have to listen to you.—Virginia.

We've enjoyed tremendously *Women's Adornment*. Please send us one more dozen.—(church) Indiana.

I have used your book in our young married couple's class. I know you don't claim this is the final or complete answer to all questions, but, as I have told some, this is the best explanation I have seen. I will hold this view until a better one comes along.—(pastor) Arkansas.

I cannot tell you what a tremendous blessing this book has been to me. Several members of our congregation have expressed a desire to have a copy of their own after reading the one I have. I am happy to oblige them, because I know that careful study of the issues you address will be enlightening to them. God bless you in your ministry! —(pastor) Texas.

About one year ago I read your book on women's adornment and found out a lot of things that really liberated my wife and I and brought us out of some tight and strict bondage....It sure is good to have the Holy Ghost and be free from the doctrines and commandments of men. —Kansas.